FLAWED

How Your Financial World Is Systematically Being
Confiscated Without Any Evidence Of A Crime.

**It's A Wicked,
Wicked Game.**

Leonard A. Renier

Wealth & Wisdom Institute Inc.
www.wealthandwisdominc.com

Leonard Renier

ACKNOWLEDGEMENTS

There are people in my life, who have influenced me and my way of thinking. My wife, Janice is the miracle in my life. Her love and support gives me the energy to seek out the best that I can be. My children, Jacqui, Colleen, Beth and Zeb are with me every day in my heart and mind.

The people that influenced and expanded my knowledge have played an important role in my life, but much of my passion comes from the professionals across the country that personally touched my life. They are committed, dedicated and have the gift to change people's lives.

At Wealth & Wisdom Institute I am also fortunate to be surrounded by very good people in my office. They are the best and remind me daily what America is all about. Life is good when you enjoy what you are doing.

CONTENTS

It's Time To Talk...1

It's a Wicked, Wicked Game...3
    The Monetary Unit

The Defining Moment In Your Thought Process......................6

The Process Of Making Financial Decisions...........................8

Your Retirement Party..14

From The Very Beginning..15
    The Financial Formula

Spreadsheet-Illustrations..19
    Graphs & Charts

The Future Is Not What It Use To Be...................................23

Government Challenges...27
    Shaping Your Financial Future

Economic Trends & Shifts..28

Perception Or Deception...30

Leverage..37

Rules Of The Rich..38

Wealth & Wisdom Institute..44

Solving The Problem...47

Leonard Renier

I cannot change the course of government actions
..But
I can prepare you for what is about to happen.

I have joined a growing group of professionals from across the country who are deeply concerned about the direction we are headed and the impact it will have on everyone's life.

As a member of Wealth & Wisdom Institute, I would like to share with you opportunities that may be right in front of you that you don't see. These opportunities are so critical to your future I feel I have an obligation to share this information with you. It's ok to say, no thanks, but I don't want to be another person in your life to rob you of these opportunities as others have done in the past. I believe that, in sharing information and knowledge, you will be able to make better life decisions.

Knowledge is something you learn; Wisdom is the ability to apply that knowledge to your everyday life.

Respectfully,

America...It's time to talk.

It's time to talk openly and honestly. This is not meant to be a lecture, sales pitch, or a rant blaming one group or another. This is meant to be a discussion about your life, your financial life, and how it is systematically being confiscated without any evidence of a crime. The perpetrators who are making your life difficult are also the ones who control the rules and continually put you at risk. Then, the same people who are causing the problems go about advising you how you should live your life.

With over 30 years of experience in the financial services industry, I must confess to you that I don't believe in traditional financial thinking and the way it's being sold to the public. It is not a science, if it were a science, then no one should lose money. The results of traditional planning lie somewhere between hope and hopelessness. The problem with this planning approach is that common sense keeps getting in the way of this type of thinking.

You must understand that we are all involved in the evolution of transferring away most of our wealth to those who create the situations, control the outcome and profit from it. Yet most Americans continue to rely on the steadiness and trustworthiness of the government and the financial services industry to guide us to our futures.

Unfortunately, these two groups create the most transfers of wealth in your life.

In many ways, the financial services industry continues to embrace the "product", not wisdom. Knowledge is something you learn; Wisdom is the ability to apply that knowledge to your everyday life. The problem is, traditional thinking continues to focus on planning goals 20 to 30 years from now, while most Americans are looking for answers that can impact their lives in the next 20 to 30 days. In traditional thinking, you will quickly learn that stability, in long term planning, is often an illusion and you will soon discover that "hope" is not a good strategy.

Today, the financial services industry should be engaging people with information that will impact their everyday lives. It should be discussing the elements that will change their financial futures that traditional financial products cannot solve.

Not long ago, from a distance, the financial services industry stood by and watched people lose their homes and many of their retirement dreams. In that historical moment, everyone discovered our lack of understanding about economic trends and shifts and how those trends and shifts impact people's lives.

The reality is the only thing traditional thinking and planning can clearly predict are the financial losses people face in the future due to taxes, inflation and the depreciation in the buying power of the dollar. Many of the financial products being sold today do not solve the problems of taxes, inflation and value of the dollar that the average American faces. In many ways traditional planning is simply an effort to earn more money than people are about to lose.

Unfortunately, the average American household is undisciplined, unready and in many cases unaware of the challenges they are facing and that they are involved in the battle for their future, a battle many fear they may be losing.

IT'S A WICKED, WICKED GAME

From the very beginning, you need to discover that your personal financial world is a wicked, wicked game. The difficulty of getting ahead and or maintaining your lifestyle may not be caused by you but are buried deep in traditional financial thinking.

First of all, I get paid with a monetary unit for the work that I do. The problem is that, historically, the longer I hold this monetary unit over a period of time, the less value or buying power it has. You need to understand this clearly and remember it always.

Unfortunately, when I get paid, government entities, who created the monetary units, tax me on the number of monetary units I receive for the work I've done. So now,

not only do I lose 10%, 20%, 30%, or more of my monetary units to government taxes, the longer I hold the monetary units I have left, the less value they have.

Now, I need to purchase goods and services to provide for my family. The problem is that the cost of these goods and services continue to increase. So after paying taxes, I have less monetary units, and due to cost increases, that monetary unit buys less goods and services. Just when I think somehow I will survive these problems I realize that government entities are also taxing many of the purchases I make. These taxes and cost increases actually reduce the amount of goods and services I can afford.

As I am standing in line to purchase some of these goods for my family, I begin to think that the companies who manufacture and provide the goods and services are also taxed by government entities for the work that they do. But these companies are smart; they take their tax burden and add it to the price of their goods and services that I buy.

Leonard Renier

I start to realize I am involved in a wicked game.

I go to work and earn monetary units (dollars) and I get taxed by the government entity on the number of monetary units I earn.

The longer I keep these monetary units, over a period of time, the less value they have.

The goods and services that I purchase, in most cases, are also taxed by government entities.

The cost of goods and services I purchase continue to go up in the price as the value of my monetary units goes down.

Finally, the goods and services I purchase are used up, need to be replaced and / or depreciate over time.

I have to ask myself, who invented this game? Well, the answer is this game was created by those who create the situation, control the outcome and profit from it.

Before you do anything in the financial life, you must first understand how money actually works in your life. You must learn how the wicked, wicked game is played in order to find the right financial solutions.

A DEFINING MOMENT IN YOUR THOUGHT PROCESS

In traditional financial thinking, you are being told "what to think" instead of "how to think" from a variety of different sources. For some Americans, this process of traditional thinking has resulted in a life filled with distress, distrust, and disappearing dreams in their financial lives. There is a need to develop a new understanding and discover a thought process that will help you survive today's economic challenges.

There are two defining moments you must learn that impact your decision making process.

First,

Your money will never be worth more than it is today.

At three percent inflation, a thousand dollars today will have the buying power of four hundred and eleven dollars thirty years from now.

Second,

The current tax bracket you are in now may be the lowest tax bracket you will be in for the rest of your life.

Due to economic trends and shifts such as; a declining workforce, an aging population, people living longer on more government programs and uncontrollable government debt, your taxes will most likely continue to increase far into the future.

So let us combine the two defining moments. Your money will never be worth more than it is today. And the current tax bracket you are in may be the lowest tax bracket you will be in for the rest of your life. Why is traditional thinking telling you to take as many of today's dollars that you can and hold them as long as you can into the future, where those dollars will have less buying power and be taxed the most? How long do you want to continue to do that?

I want you to take a dollar out of your pocket, look at it and remember, the longer I hold this monetary unit, the less value it has.

This issue of holding a monetary unit and the loss of its value over time is in direct conflict with traditional financial thinking and planning. Traditional thinking believes the center point of success is holding on to these monetary units and accumulating them far into the future. The problem is accumulation growth does not equal value growth over a period of time. So from the very beginning, the traditional thought process of accumulation is flawed. If a process is flawed from the very beginning, how accurate are results going to be in the future?

THE PROCESS OF MAKING FINANCIAL DECISIONS

For the average American, everyday financial decisions are being shaped by five elements that surround their everyday lives. These five elements control and determine their lifestyles and the way they live. Many Americans are unaware how much influence these elements have in their everyday decision making process.

The five elements or problems the average American faces are:

- Risk
- Taxes
- Penalties – Regulation
- Inflation
- Value of the Dollar

It is here, in these five elements or problems, where the average American's decision making process becomes paralyzed and mistakes happen. Then, with the help of the government and the financial services industry, the problems start to compound into what may become even larger problems in the future. If these five elements or problems exist in your life you must ask yourself a very simple question. Does traditional thinking and planning really solve these five problems I have? Many times, traditional thinking believes they have solutions for some of the problems you have, but many of their solutions have the same problems you should be avoiding.

What you may discover, as I did, is that inside the design of many financial products being sold today, there is no assurity of success. In reality, what will determine the success of a financial product are the economic trends and shifts that will impact that product's results. This may be the reason why you will find so many disclaimers in every financial product.

Traditional planning comes along and says we can help you solve the problems you face of risk, taxes, penalties-regulations, inflation, and the value of the dollar. All you need is a qualified plan or some type of brokerage investment account.

Maybe you will need some mutual funds or bank CDs, perhaps an annuity or some kind of mortgage reduction plan. But, the question is, do any of these solve the five problems you face? The reality is 'no'. What is going to determine the risk you feel you need to take to survive in the future, the taxes you must pay, the penalties or regulations on the things you buy or own, the inflation and the cost in your everyday life and the value or buying power of your dollar? The Government. The problem is not too many people in the financial services industry are paying attention to how the actions of the government could crush everyone's financial future.

Let's test some of the solutions and recommendations traditional thinking offers up in traditional planning. Does a traditional IRA or 401K solve your problems of risk, taxes, penalties-regulations, inflation and the value of a dollar? No.

What, in the last ten years, has the financial services industry done to improve your financial future?

You might even come to the conclusion that a traditional IRA or 401K contains all of the problems you don't want. Does a bank CD or some type of mutual fund solve the problems? In these cases, did traditional thinking solve the problem you face or did their solutions compound the same problems in the future? Remember, the longer you hold these monetary units, the less value they have.

Perhaps you are now beginning to realize that you are involved in a wicked, wicked game. You may also begin to realize that some of your financial difficulties and challenges are not caused by you. They are the direct result of following processes that do not solve the real problems you face. Remember, in many ways you are involved in the evolution of transferring away most of your wealth to those who create the situations, control the outcomes and profit from it.

So what, if anything, has the financial services industry done to improve the average American's life? Over the last fifty years, the financial industry has served up a variety of products and programs. It is important for you to remember that in the design of financial products, inside the product itself, there is no assurity of success. What is really going to determine the success of the financial products you have are the economic trends and shifts at the time you use them.

Economic changes, taxes, risk, penalties-regulations, inflation and the value of the dollar will determine a product's success. The problem is traditional thinking continues to focus on the products they sell with very little interest in understanding economic trends and shifts that will impact the future.

Let's, once again, test traditional thinking. Another center point of traditional thinking is to defer taxes to a later date. If you knew the Federal Government received $1.4 trillion in income taxes in fiscal year 2012 and the government's own prediction is a 75% increase in income tax revenues in the next five years, would you still believe it is a good idea to defer taxes to a later date? Without having this economic information, how can anyone make a financial recommendation or decision? Why weren't these economic trends shared with you? Do you think this information will impact your retirement income? Should your financial goal be to defer taxes to a later date or try to avoid the taxation if possible? Remember, the longer you hold the monetary unit, the less value it has.

Does deferring taxes solve the five problems you face? Traditional thinking may have you looking for answers in all the wrong places. It's a wicked, wicked game.

YOUR RETIREMENT PARTY

The buying power of your dollar and the element of time are the most important factors in any planning process. Now, I need to introduce you to people that you don't want to invite to your retirement party, Mr. Inflation, Mr. Taxation, and Mr. Depreciation.

If you took $100 today and put it into a typical qualified plan for your retirement....and you believe you could get a 5% rate of return over the next 30 years...you would end up with about $446. Now you are ready to retire and here come the party poopers. Mr. Taxation wants about 20% or more of your $446. The buying power twins Mr. Inflation and Mr. Depreciation have each quietly taken about 3% of your money each and every year. Wait a minute, 30 years ago you put in $100 of buying power. Thirty years later, even though you earned 5% each year, you met Mr. Inflation, Mr. Depreciation, and Mr. Taxation and you end up with about $62 of buying power at that time. That's 38% less buying power than when you started 30 years ago. Now comes a simple, common sense question. When do you want to take money out of a qualified retirement plan? When taxes are the highest or the lowest? Will taxes be higher or lower in the future? You see, it can be a wicked, wicked game.

FROM THE VERY BEGINNING

TIME x RATE OF RETURN x MONETARY UNIT = ACCUMULATION

Once again, if, from the very beginning, the premise or the formulas for calculating a result is incorrect, how accurate are the results going to be? What seems like forever, traditional financial thinking has used the formula of: Time X Rate of Return X the Number of Monetary Units = Accumulation in calculating future value. Remember, the monetary unit is failing to hold its value and buying power, yet is the center point of this calculation. Let's examine some of the flaws in this planning formula that will most definitely impact your financial future.

TIME

In the traditional thinking formula, time is the only true measurement in this formula yet when dealing with someone's life, the length of someone's life is unpredictable. In this formula, the consistency of time is unlike the consistency of rates of return and the consistency of the value of the monetary unit. The flaw is that you can't make up time once it has been lost or spent. Your time is the most precious asset you have. In traditional thinking, if you have no time then all of the other aspects of the formula won't work. So if you suffer a financial loss in one year, that one year dramatically changes the results at the end of the calculation. If you do suffer a loss financially in any particular year, the typical reaction is that you will have to get higher rates of return the following year to make up for the losses but this solution also takes time.

RATE OF RETURN

The second element in the traditional thinking formula is rate of return. There are a couple of flaws associated with rates of return that will impact results. The first flaw is that people often use the stock market as a vehicle to produce rates of return and the stock market is very inconsistent. There is very little certainty in the market. Since 1929, about 31% of the time, the DOW Jones Industrial Average has recorded negative year end results. Not only is this a loss of money but also a loss of time. There is also an inconsistency in the way the DOW is measured. It is measured on the volume and there is no correlation between volume in the market and the increased numbers of dollars in circulations by the Federal Reserve. Rates of return can also be manipulated by government regulation, taxation and or actions taken by the Federal Reserve. If the DOW experiences negative year end results 31% of the time, the average American working 40 years could experience a down market ten to twelve years in that 40 year cycle. That's ten to twelve years of time that can't be made up.

Recognizing the difference between real financial opportunities and some company's sales goals will be difficult.

MONETARY UNITS (MONEY)

The third element of the traditional thinking formula is monetary units better known as money. Without money there can be no accumulation. But the flaw of our monetary unit or money is its instability. The longer I hold this monetary unit or money, the less buying power or value it has. Much of traditional planning is done with a model where the value of the monetary unit remains stable yet we live in a world that is filled with inflation and depreciation of the dollar. The results of inflation and depreciation make maintaining your lifestyle a moving target and harder to achieve. The everyday loss of value in the monetary unit makes it harder to replace the goods and services we want and need with depreciating monetary units. Many Americans are finding it difficult maintaining their current lifestyles and this is a direct result of the changing economic trends and shifts.

ACCUMULATION

The final element in the traditional thinking formula represents the results of the TIME X RATE OF RETURN X MONETARY UNIT process. But the major flaw with accumulation is the accumulation does not represent value or buying power. Another flaw in accumulation is that it does not anticipate any taxes, inflation, depreciation or government regulations that rob the monetary unit of its value. In the traditional thinking formula, the only element that can be measured or predicted accurately is the element of time.

SPREADSHEETS – ILLUSTRATIONS – GRAPHS AND CHARTS

-ALWAYS IN QUESTION NEVER IN DOUBT-

The formula of TIME X RATE OF RETURN X MONETARY UNIT = ACCUMULATION can be presented to you in a variety of graphs, spreadsheets and illustrations. In many cases, even though these assumptions lack certainty, traditional thinkers continue to use them. Companies who use these spreadsheets to estimate future results, use disclaimers holding themselves harmless of any inaccuracies. They seem more convinced of these spreadsheets inaccuracies than accuracies. If that is true, why does the entire financial service industry continue to use them when they are based on a mathematical formula that is not precise from the very beginning? If the formula or premise is not accurate from the very beginning how precise will the results be in the future? Remember, all of this is done with a monetary unit that the longer you hold on to it, the less value it has.

SPREADSHEETS – ILLUSTRATIONS – GRAPHS AND CHARTS

THE PROBLEM MASQUERADING AS THE SOLUTION

Many times after a spreadsheet, illustration, or written plan is given to you it contains disclaimers such as this....

"Spreadsheet models are provided without any expressed or implied warranties whatsoever. They do not represent legal, tax, investment, insurance, financial or accounting advice. If such advice is required, the appropriate professional should be consulted. The spreadsheet models may not be suitable for every individual and are not guaranteed or warranted to produce any particular results. Additionally, no warranty is made regarding the accuracy of the content, and the user must assume the entire risk of acting on anything therein."

Really?! Sounds like a good plan to me. Where do I sign up? The reality is there probably wouldn't be a need for a disclaimer if financial products dealt in certainty. But, many of the products in the financial services industry deal in risk, taxes, regulation, inflation, and the value of the dollar. The industry is not good at making you aware of the economic trends and shifts that could or will impact the results of the products and plans they are presenting.

So for a moment, let's pretend that all these spreadsheets are right. Let's pretend all the company's illustrations are correct. If that is true, then it would be very easy to find and buy future financial success.

As a planner for many years, I decided a while back to review client cases from fifteen to twenty years ago. What I was looking for was how accurate initial assumptions were compared to results today. The painful reality was that the spreadsheets and illustrations were not very accurate. These results were not because of poor planning and bad products, it was because the economic trends and shift changed dramatically. Risk, taxes, regulation, inflation, and depreciation of the dollar crushed the plans of the past.

INFORMATION

-A SURE THING-

Look at it this way. If you knew for certain a particular stock was going to skyrocket in value, would you invest in it? Now, if you knew income taxes were going to increase dramatically in the next ten years would you still believe it was a good idea to defer taxes to a later date when taxes would be higher?

**Your financial future will not
be determined by the product alone.
What will determine the success are the
economic trends and shifts that surround
that product at that time.**

THE FUTURE IS NOT WHAT IT USE TO BE

The problem is there are two basic elements that are missing elements in traditional financial thinking and planning. They are economic trends and shifts and the concept of leverage. Both of these elements will have a direct impact on your future financial results.

THE DEVASTATING IMPACT ON YOUR FINANCIAL SUCCESS

What you know today will determine where you will be financially five to 10 years from now. The products available to you in the financial world will not make you smarter simply by purchasing them. Success can be achieved only when you understand how these products impact your future. Will these products solve the problems of taxes, risk, inflation, penalties and the value of the dollar, or simply compound the same problems in the future? The challenge is to avoid as many future problems as you can.

The flaw in traditional thinking is the belief that simply purchasing a financial product assures some type of success. But, products over a period of time do not adjust with trends and shifts in the economy. The question is, who or what will impact the trends and shifts in the economy? Who or what will have a direct impact on the problems you face in the future? The government.

The government will determine your future financial success. The government controls the elements of the economy that determine the success of the financial products you purchase. The government's actions will determine future taxes in your life. The government controls elements of inflation, which is determined by the amount of money they print. It is the government that controls the penalties and regulations on industries and the financial products you purchase. Government actions also impact the financial marketplace, which could create substantial risk to individual investors. It is the government's actions that ultimately depreciate the value of the dollar worldwide. No product can solve these problems. Without having some knowledge of economic trends and shifts, buying financial products could be an aimless shot in the dark.

Let's measure the impact the government has on the problems you want to avoid and how these problems will limit your financial success and growth in the future. The government has selected the option of continuing to feed the problems they face in the future. Their solution is to simply throw more money at the problem ... your money. The government's problem is that they need more revenue (taxes) from a declining workforce, an aging population and citizens that have an inability to save and invest for their futures. The government has direct control over the problems you face, so it may be fair to say that your financial future is connected to the financial success of the government.

The real success of any financial product will be directly affected by the challenges that the government faces. The unsolved mysteries of the Federal Government will impact government spending, debt and the ability to collect the taxes needed to pay for these challenges. The government's only source of revenue is to collect taxes and oversee the printing of more money. Both of their solutions will create problems for you. Taxes on investments, savings, property and purchases will reduce your spendable income. Simply printing more money could create inflation, increase the price of goods you buy and decrease the value of your hard-earned money. To compensate for these government solutions, you may have to reduce your standard of living.

THE COST OF NOT SOLVING THE PROBLEM

No problem can be solved by blaming another person. The cure for cancer will not be found if researchers simply blame each other for not achieving results. Spending more money on research, without finding a cure, does not solve the problem.

25

The reason the Titanic sunk was not the fault of the iceberg. It was the course and the speed of the ship that particular evening. Everyone knew that icebergs in the Atlantic were not uncommon. But the tragic results of that night go all the way back to how the ship was designed and built and that the captain and crew were not prepared for a crisis of that magnitude.

The same can be said why personal financial challenges will continue to haunt the average American. Finding a cure for financial ailments will be difficult without understanding the root cause of the disease.

The role of the government will impact your personal financial future. Their inability to solve problems they face will continue to cost us personally. In discussing these challenges, the goal is not to blame any political party or blame any president, as the media does. These are serious problems that need to be solved. This is not a popularity contest.

ESSENTIAL LESSON
GOVERNMENT CHALLENGES AND UNSOLVED MYSTERIES THAT WILL SHAPE YOUR FINANCIAL FUTURE

The role of the government will impact everyone's financial future. The approach the government uses when it is faced with a problem has been to simply spend more money on the problem to fix it. The government is a big believer in feeding the problem, not solving the problem. The cost of government and its programs continues to escalate. The pace at which government is growing surpasses the cost of inflation and the growth of the average American's income. The government continues to avoid the challenges and tough choices that need to be made. Politicians continue to offer "free" government programs in exchange for votes with no personal liability for the cost of the programs. It is important to shed some light on the problems and challenges the government faces and how they will impact you personally, financially and our country as a whole.

THE BATTLE FOR OUR FUTURE

The challenges of the Federal Government go beyond political party lines. The accumulation of political mistakes, corruption and greed over the years has decayed our country. Simply blaming one side or another is another form of FEEDING THE PROBLEM, NOT SOLVING THE PROBLEM.

We must also recognize that there are individuals in our country that would be happy if the country collapsed in order to fulfill their agenda. Here are some of the Unsolved Mysteries that our country and government are facing and the financial impact it will have on you.

ECONOMIC TRENDS AND SHIFTS THE DEVISTATING INPACT ON YOUR FUTURE

For years now, the Government Accountability Office (GAO) has warned every one of the most obvious economic trends. They report that America faces a declining workforce, an aging population living longer on more government programs and a smaller working class that has an inability to save. These economic and demographic trends do not spell success for the future.

The GAO report goes on to say that the debt and spending of the Federal Government is unsustainable into the future and that the government has no options but to raise taxes (real taxes or through government regulations) or reduce benefits or both.

Other economic and demographic trends will impact future results of your personal financial planning. The cost of expanding government dependency programs supported by fewer taxpaying workers. Government dependency is now a generational problem that not only increases the government's debt but also your tax liability. The cost of going "green" in our country was underestimated by almost 300%. The cost of health care is over 200% of what it was first projected with more cost increases (or less benefits) to come. The cost of underfunded government and union pensions. The Government Accountability Office and the Congressional Budget Office (CBO) has been unable to report the cost of illegal and legal immigration. The declining value and buying power of the American dollar and inflation in the cost and manufacturing (regulations) of goods you use to support your everyday lifestyle. Speaking of regulations, recently thousands of new regulations have been imposed by the government. As a tax paying citizen, can you name three of them?

All of these economic trends and shifts are certain to impact your financial future yet remain a missing element, a factor, in addressing your financial future. In traditional thinking these issues are not on their spreadsheets or illustrations. So how are you to prepare if these trends are not discussed? How can anyone make a recommendation or a decision without first having economic trend and shift information? In traditional thinking, all the risk belongs to you. That is probably why there are so many disclaimers in the financial services industry.

When the government started and continued to print more money, it was easy to predict that the stock market would go up in volume. But, here is the problem; the volume in the market place has outpaced the value of the dollar. We should start to view the dollar as a tax certificate for the government. The government gets a portion of each dollar they print through taxes. So if you were them, would you print more? By printing more dollars their tax revenues increase. But printing more dollars creates inflation and less buying power or value to you. You may also discover that the market place volume can be manipulated by government regulations, bailouts of industries, dependency programs and a number of creative concepts. It's a wicked, wicked game.

ASKING A SIMPLE QUESTION, IS IT PERCEPTION OR DECEPTION?

Happy days are here again; at least that is what we are being told. Epictetus Phrygian, a philosopher, in 108 AD reminds us that there are four kinds of appearances....

1) Things are as they appear to be
2) Things neither are or appear to be
3) Things are, but do not appear to be
4) Things are not, yet appear to be

For now, I would like to discuss number four, things are not, yet appear to be. You can decide whether or not what you are being told about the economy is perception or deception.

THE STOCK MARKET

The perception is the stock market is at record highs (2014 time frame) therefore the economy is great. Everyone wants their investments to gain in value. Four years ago, I told everyone I met that the market was going to go up. I must be a genius, right?

No. But I was aware that the Federal Reserve and the government were going to significantly increase the number of printed dollars in circulation. On their website the Federal Reserve of St. Louis reports that in the year 2000, there were $571 billion dollars in circulation. In the year 2000 the high for the DOW Industrial Average was 11,313. The feds now report (2014) there is over $1.25 trillion in circulation, almost a 125% increase. So if in the year 2000, $571 billion supported an 11,300 point DOW, today with over $1.2 trillion in circulation, using the same equation as in 2000; the DOW should be around 25,000 points. If the Federal Reserve and the government decided today to double the amount of printed money, would the DOW go up even more? So is market success being manipulated by the actions of the Federal Reserve and the government?

The Federal Reserve and the government have also been actively involved in Quantitative Easoning. Simply put, supplementing dollars into the market place because of an uncertain economy. Perception or Deception?

INFLATION

The government reports that inflation is only at about 1.5%. This is truly great news for everyone. It proves that maintaining your lifestyle is clearly manageable. Perception or deception? Well, first of all, you must understand that the government in many of its social and dependency programs increase the dollars in these programs every year by the inflation factor or CPI. So their goal is to keep these increases at a minimum.

In the early 1980s inflation was measured by a variety of economic factors. Since then, the Consumer Price Index (CPI) has been reconfigured by the government to underestimate the inflation factor. The CPI no longer measures the cost of maintaining your standard of living. According to John Williams and the Shadow Government, the CPI no longer measures full inflation of everyday costs. With the measure of academic theory, politicians have significantly underreported real inflation. Politicians continue to reduce the number of economic factors that measure inflation. This underreporting impairs the ability of retirees, income earners and investors to stay ahead of inflation. Underestimating inflation has created the illusion of a recovering and growing economy. If the inflation factors of the 1980s were used to measure inflation today, the inflation factor would be almost 9%, not the 1% to 2% reported by the government. Perhaps this is why you are finding it difficult to maintain your everyday lifestyle.

ECONOMICS, GOVERNMENT, COMPANY GOALS

Flawed from its foundation, economics as a whole has failed to improve much with time. As it developed into an academic establishment and mutated into mathematics, the Newtonian Scheme has become an illusion of determinism in a changing, tempestuous world of human actions. Economists became preoccupied with mechanical models of markets and uninterested in the willful people who inhabit them.

George Gilder, Knowledge and Power – The Inflation Theory of Capitalism and How It Is Revolutionizing Our World

Many economists believe, as many other "scientific studies" believe, the problem is not their theory; the problem is that the real world is not responding correctly to their theory, therefore the real world is the problem.

The real problem is a particularly true theory or formula, using selected data to achieve desired "scientific" results, will constantly have to adjust its "truths" to maintain the perception that its "science" is correct.

Buried deep underneath the surface, the role of government, its regulations, and manipulations of financial markets is creating unintended consequences that will impact everyone's financial future.

The current economic policy allows politicians to avoid making the necessary decisions needed to improve future financial growth for people and to correct the damage they are overseeing to our children's future.

The role of the financial services industry, which is consumed by government regulations and dogged by, in many ways, self inflicted compliance rules, primarily is motivated by and for profit. Many professionals in the financial services industry have the luxury of not knowing what they should know. Many times the public can become confused between what is good sound advice and some representatives desire to be recognized by a company for their sales activity. From a distance, you can see the dilemma the public must deal with. In every aspect of your life, you are being told "what to think" not "how to think" about your financial future. This can have a paralyzing effect on your ability to make life decisions. Without more information and understanding, all the elements that can impact your financial future, recognizing the difference between real financial opportunities and some company's sales goal will be difficult.

Many economists believe, as many other "scientific studies" believe, the problem is not in their theory. The problem is that the real world is not responding correctly to their theory.

LEVERAGE

Understanding the economic trends and shifts and how certain elements such as taxes, inflation, depreciation, and the value of the dollar may lead you to think that avoiding future taxation could be a winning strategy. But traditional thinking continues to funnel you through a process of deferring taxation to a later date to where economic trends point to much higher taxation in the future.

The second element that is missing in traditional thinking is the concept of LEVERAGE. How do you get from point A to point B in your financial life without exposing yourself to risk, taxes, government regulations, inflation and the depreciating value of the dollar? If you pay off your house as fast as you can, does your house increase in value? Does paying off your car make the value of your car go up? Does overfunding your 401K make the rates of return higher? No! But the funny thing is every financial institution is telling you that's what you should be doing. What is missing in this thought process is the word LEVERAGE.

There are three different types of leverage. The first is financial leverage. Financial leverage is simply using the least amount of money to create the most amounts of wealth or benefits. There is also economic leverage. This type of leverage uses information to achieve the best possible results. An example of this type of leverage would be knowing taxes will continue to rise and the solution would be to avoid all the taxes you can. The third type of leverage is opportunity leverage. An example of this type of leverage would be me selling you a piece of property worth $50,000 for only $1000; you realize the gain right away. Opportunity leverage is an element that creates value without the factor of time.

Understanding these three types of leverage will help you avoid financial problems and will assist you in establishing new financial strategies.

RULES OF THE RICH

For years the rich have understood the process of gaining and controlling wealth. They also have discovered ways of transferring their wealth to the next generation of their family. The rich follow three basic principles or rules when seeking to create wealth.

Rule Number 1

Use the least amount of money to create the most amount of wealth.

Rule Number 2

Guarantee the wealth will occur and the money will transfer tax free.

Rule Number 3

Create multiples of wealth immediately.

How does this thinking compare to the traditional thought process today? How many of the financial products that you own meet the rules of the rich? How many products do you have that actually have the three types of leverage attached to them? And finally, what product or financial plans do you have that solve the problems of risk, taxes, regulation, inflation and the declining value of your dollar?

ENLISTING NEW STRATEGIES

What you may, or may not know, is that everything in your life has value. You may own a home and a car, have a bank saving program, a 401K or IRA, you may own stocks or bonds, mutual funds, annuities, gold and silver, CDs, real estate, a business, you may have a family, some type of inheritance and life insurance. The big question is of all these things you have, which of them can you drive forward or increase the value of today? Which of these assets solve the problem of risk, taxes, regulation, inflation and depreciation of the dollar? Look at the list again, which of these assets have any of the three types of leverage attached to them. Your new strategy should focus on creating leverage whenever you can. What financial elements in your life empower leverage? Understanding the three types of leverage could help you gather future dollars without taxation, create wealth without the element of time and find consistency and stability without risk.

START vs. FINISH

Almost every American has dreams of retirement and some ideas of creating a comfortable life in the future. Most Americans know how they want to finish life. Very few know how to get there. Traditional thinking and planning has failed many and, in the process, destroyed dreams of a lifetime. Many problems of reaching goals in the future are caused by a lack of information and a sound financial understanding. Getting to the finish line is not the goal because everyone will finish. How they finish will be determined by "the start and the preparation" of getting to the finish line. If everyone is going to finish, then the difference between finishing successfully or poorly will be determined in the strategy of running the race.

YOUR APPROACH

Everything you do in life and the results of your actions will depend upon how you prepare. If you wanted to become a doctor, you wouldn't prepare by studying all the art courses you could in college, would you? No, unless of course you were interested in having the fanciest waiting room in the world. To be a doctor, you would study all the appropriate courses and then enter into medical school.

Your money is no different. You need to apply a thought process to where you want to be in your financial future. Heading into that future without a clue of how your money works will expose you to many unintended consequences. Now is the time to understand how your money works and discover all of the opportunities that may be right in front of you. The defining moment in your life will occur when you are no longer "out of control" in your financial life.

Analyzing and understanding your financial situation will give you a clearer view of the opportunities you have and will guide you in making better life decisions in the future.

THE INNOCENT AMERICAN BYSTANDER

It is becoming more and more apparent that the average American is being crushed in a wicked, wicked economic game. Between the lack of understanding about leverage (using the least amount of money to create the most amount of wealth) in current financial solutions and the expanding amount of government regulations, taxes, and control over your everyday financial decisions, the average American has become a casualty of others greed and power. Unfortunately the two groups who profess to have your best interest in mind, the government and financial services industry, are the ones who stand to benefit the most. So while you are sitting there, minding your own business, efforts by others to confiscate your financial future continue.

LOOKING FOR ANSWERS IN ALL THE WRONG PLACES

As we have discussed, if you're starting out with a process or formula that is flawed from the very beginning, how accurate are the results going to be? It will be difficult to get the right solution when you are starting out with the wrong premise. Solutions in your financial world come in two formats, things you should be doing and things you shouldn't be doing. So the question remains, how can anyone make recommendations without understanding the economic trends and shifts that will impact your future?

So while you are sitting there minding your own business, efforts to confiscate your financial future continue.

WEALTH AND WISDOM INSTITUTE

As a planner, I started to realize there were elements in the financial world that were taking shape. In the 90s technology drove the stock market, the government wanted to make sure everyone owned a home and Fannie Mae and Freddie Mac were the government's tool to make sure almost everyone qualified for a mortgage. At the same time, housing prices soared. Investment companies started using mortgage debt as an investment tool for the public to invest in. No one seemed to realize that all of this growth was debt driven. The government started to realign how they measured inflation and government debt continued at a rapid pace. Government dependency became an acceptable lifestyle and retirees were living longer on more government programs. Then terrorist attacks and war. As I looked at my own retirement spreadsheets, none of the above mentioned elements had been taken into account. I realized my spreadsheet was just math and assumptions imputed into a computer. I also started to realize what I thought to be true in the financial world was not true. I decided to start to research economic trends and shifts that would impact everyone's financial future. The results were eye opening.

Many professionals in the financial- services business have the luxury of not knowing what they should know. You see, they cannot be aware of something they are not aware of. Some professionals in this industry have it all wrong: they have difficulty getting beyond the product solution. The solution is about you, the people, not the company's product of the month or their ranking in a sales contest. Many times, you could become confused between what is good sound advice and someone's desire to be recognized by a company for their sales activity. From a distance, you can see the dilemma that the public must deal with. In every aspect of your life, from the media, left – or right-wing politics, and even some religions, you are being told what to think, not how to think. This has a paralyzing effect on the average person's ability to make necessary life decisions. Information and a decision-making thought process are required to make such decisions. Knowledge does not become wisdom simply because it is learned. Wisdom is the ability to apply knowledge to your everyday life. Without a thought process or a guide in your decision making, recognizing the difference between an opportunity in your life and a company's sales goals will be difficult.

I formed Wealth & Wisdom Institute as a research and training center to reach out to other advisors in the financial services industry to help get information to the public. The purpose of the Institute was educational based without financial company or product endorsements. The

Institute is focused on ETS, economic trends and shifts that would impact your future. Representatives who are members of the Institute have the advantage in discussing with you some of the realities in today's financial world.

An integral piece of your financial future is working with a competent advisor. The professional you choose to work with should be a true advocate of your dreams, hopes and goals. An advocate is someone who will defend and support you and not the goals of a financial company. A true advocate will have the beliefs, morals and ethics that you believe in. True advocacy is centered on lasting relationships. Within that relationship, the advisor should take the role of an educator. As an educator, your advisor's focus should be on teaching you how to think, instead of telling you what to think. Your advocate and advisor should be knowledgeable on the economic trends and shifts that will impact your financial future. They should be willing to challenge traditional thinking. Your advocate must be knowledgeable and a specialist when discussing the role of your family and should prepare you for the challenges of the future. View your selection of an advocate as a long term relationship. His role also includes communicating the importance of your everyday financial decisions. With more knowledge, you will be able to make better life decisions. Choosing the right professional should be considered an opportunity of a lifetime, so choose wisely.

Today, there is a growing group of professionals from across the country who are deeply concerned about the direction we are heading as a country and the impact it will have on your financial future. You must understand your economic situation is a matter of choice not a matter of chance. With more information you will be able to make better life decisions. We believe at the Institute that the financial products and plans you purchased in the past should not be the source of your knowledge but the result of your knowledge.

SOLVING THE PROBLEM

First of all, you should be congratulated for some of the decisions you have made in the past. With the information you had at the time, you probably made the best decisions you could. Now, with more information, you may want to rethink some of the decisions you have made in the past.

Just about every attempt to accumulate future dollars will involve the elements of risk, taxes, penalties and government regulations. Your future dollars will also lose buying power due to inflation and depreciation of the dollar.

The first step in solving the problem is to understand the wicked game that is being played. Next, you need to discover that almost everything in your life has value.

Some typical assets may include IRA's, 401K's, stocks, mutual funds, bank savings, annuities, your home and real estate, gold, silver, and other possessions you may have. Make a list of your assets. In listing your assets, you should also consider some non-traditional assets such as the value of your family. You must begin to view your family, including parents and grandparents, as a possible financial entity. You should consider possible inheritances inside the family unit. The value of your family should be insured and assured into the future. The rich have been doing this forever and consider this planning pivotal to their financial success. The rich understand that if the financial success of the family is assured in the future that they can live the best life they can, today.

The first step to any plan is to understand the assets that are at your disposal and how to use them as tools to build your financial future. All too often, financial products can be disguised as the solutions in your financial life. You must understand that everything in your life has value, and you must discover the assets in your life you control and can drive forward. It is important to discover and list all your assets.

**Having the wrong discussion
will not lead you to the right solution.**

After all, how can you get to where you want to go when you don't know where you're at?

Many Americans unknowingly and unnecessarily, transfer away much of their wealth. Once again, taxes, risks, penalties, inflation and depreciation of the dollar are major concerns everyone's efforts to maintain their lifestyles and plan for the future. These elements are difficult to control. But there are other aspects of your life that you do, and can, control. The way that your money flows in and out of your life many times are based on choices that you have made. Understand that if you have the power to make these choices, you may also have the power to change your choices. What will determine the choices you make will be a direct result of what you know at the time of your decision. With more information, knowledge and understanding of the economic trends and shifts that will impact your life, and finally discovering how money works in your life, you may want to rethink some of the decisions you made in the past. Recapturing transfers of wealth in your life will be a direct result of what you know about how money works. Wisdom is recognizing changes need to be made.

After listing all your assets, study them carefully. Many of them contain transfers of wealth, taxes, fees, charges, penalties, interest, risk of loss, etc. It is very possible to eliminate many of these transfers in your life now and in your future. If you understand the elements that are hurting you financially, then you can avoid them and recapture money that you are giving away, unknowingly and unnecessarily.

ASSET ANALYSIS

Now that you have your list of assets, I need you to take three minutes of your time to complete a survey. If you had the ability to create the most perfect investment for yourself, what would it look like? Answer the twelve questions below, yes or no.

- Would you want to have a lot of risk involved?
- Would you like to have some guarantees in it?
- Would you attach a lot of penalties in your most perfect investment?
- Would you want to get to your money whenever you needed it?
- Would you want this investment protected from creditors?
- Would you want to create the most amount of wealth or benefit using the least amount of money?
- Would you want your investment to grow tax deferred?
- Would you like the money to be distributed to you tax free?

- Would you like to use this investment as collateral for other things you wanted to do in your life?
- Would you want this investment to be tax deductable?
- If you became injured or ill and couldn't work, would you want someone to continue to deposit money into your investment?
- If you died, would you want this investment to go to your family tax free?

You have just created the most perfect investment for yourself.

Now take your list of assets that you have and one at a time and apply each one of them to the same twelve questions.

ASSET ANALYSIS – YOUR MATRIX

- Does this asset have a lot of risk involved?
- Does this asset have guarantees?
- Does this asset have penalties attached to it?
- Does this asset allow me to get to my money whenever I need it?
- Is this asset protected from creditors?
- Does this asset create the most amount of wealth or benefit using the least amount of money?
- Does this asset grow tax deferred?

- Is the money in this asset distributed to me tax-free?
- Can I use this asset as collateral for other things I want to do?
- Are my deposits in the asset tax-deductable?
- Does this asset provide for payments into my investment to continue even if I become disabled?
- In the event of my death, does this asset go to my family tax free?

You may discover that many of the assets you currently have are not as favorable as you would like them. This is a great exercise to help you discover how money works in your life. You also may now begin to understand how traditional thinking continues to "feed the problem" you face in the future, instead of actually solving the problem.

Hopefully, with all this information, you can begin to realign your thought process when it comes to your financial future. This may be a great opportunity to have an in depth discussion with your trusted advisor about your assets, transfers of wealth and avoiding financially painful economic trends and shifts. With the right conversation you may be able to recapture dollars that you are giving away unknowingly and unnecessarily. A Wealth and Wisdom Institute member will be able to discuss with you your own personal money matrix and continue your educational process.

Your education is just beginning and additional resources may be helpful in overcoming the financial challenges you face. In the future, a clear and decisive thought process will be needed. Wealth and Wisdom Institute continues to provide resources that will enhance your decision making process. Here is a summary of other Wealth and Wisdom Institute published books:

- <u>The Defining Moment</u>
  Leonard Renier   Infinity Publishing

  The Defining Moment is a 10 step approach to how money works in your life. The opportunities in life are limited to what we know, so it only makes sense to know as much as we possibly can. The key factor for successful people, in both the good and bad times, is their ability to adjust to economic situations using logic, knowledge and common sense.

  Unfortunately, many people don't get the opportunities to learn how money works in their lives. Knowing how money works is a great thing. Not knowing can be disastrous. Knowing and understanding the 10 Defining Moments is a simply process that could change your life. This book is an Infinity Publishing Best Seller.

- <u>Learning to Avoid Unintended Consequences</u>
  Leonard Renier   Infinity Publishing

  Learning to Avoid Unintended Consequences exposes the ten major transfers of wealth that can be found in the average American life. Everyone should learn and understand that many people are involved in the evolution of transferring their wealth away to those who create the situation, control the outcomes and profit from it.

  By discovering your transfers of wealth, you may have an opportunity to recapture these transfers that you are unknowingly and unnecessarily giving away. This discovery process could change everything in our problem-solving approach. This book is an Infinity Publishing Best Seller for over six years.

- <u>Sudden Impact</u>
  Leonard Renier   Infinity Publishing

  Sudden Impact discusses how certain economic and demographic events could impact your financial future.   Making financial decisions without this information may create unintended consequences in your future. Traditional financial thinking often ignores the obvious problems that will challenge your financial success.   With more economic and demographic information, you will be able to make better life decisions. This is also an Infinity Publishing Best Seller.

- <u>The Family Legacy</u>
  Leonard Renier   Infinity Publishing

  The Family Legacy is a 22 minute read, where you may discover the answers of a lifetime. Discovering the difference in the way rich people approach their financial future compared to the traditional-thinking approach is amazing. *The Family Legacy* is an opportunity to discover possible solutions in your financial future. You owe it to yourself to consider *The Family Legacy* as part of your planning process. This discussion may not be suitable for everyone, but how can you say yes or no to ideas you don't even know exist? How many opportunities will pass you by simply because you weren't aware of them?

- <u>Essential Lessons</u>
  Leonard Renier   Infinity Publishing

  Essential Lessons challenges traditional thinking and helps you discover some of the financial myths and realities that surround your everyday life. There are 25 short Essential Lesson conversations that will help you understand how money works in your life. Understanding these lessons will help you develop a new approach to your financial future.

Wealth and Wisdom Institute continues to research economic trends and demographic data that could impact your financial future. We attempt to discuss issues and we represent no industry, company or products in our discussions. It is the goal of the Institute that with more information you will be able to make better life decisions.

Visit WealthandWisdom.Institute where you will find links, articles, videos and sources of information that will continue to educate you.

You are facing the challenges of a lifetime. You're in the battle for your future and your personal financial freedom is at stake. Our ability to survive financially, survive as a family and survive as a nation is now in question. To prepare for this battle, you must gather intelligence, understand your options and have the resolve to win. Knowledge is something you learn; wisdom is the ability to apply that knowledge to your everyday life.

What you know today will determine where you will be five to ten years from now. Knowledge and wisdom are the weapons of choice to win this battle.

Flawed